dogs&us

GARETH ST JOHN THOMAS

Contents

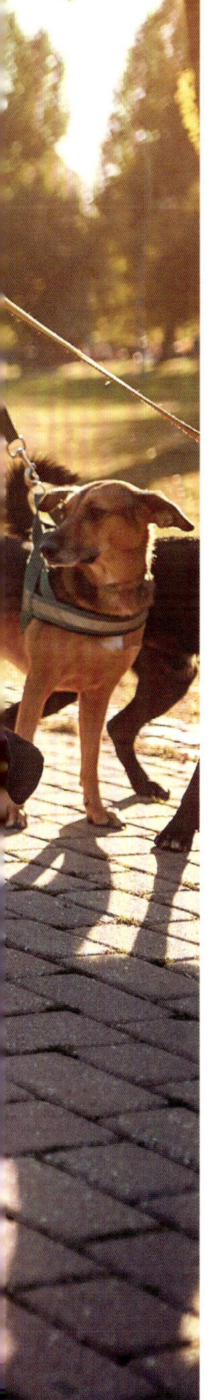

This is a book to dip in and out of at any place you choose, or even to read from cover to cover. You'll meet all sorts of dogs, sharing all of life with us. You will discover some interesting things about extraordinary breeds, and meet some real and fictional dog heroes and heroines. There is very little dogs don't do with us and for us. We find them loving and protecting our children, digging people out of an avalanche, keeping a ship's company happy, and bringing joy to the sick and lonely. We see the cutest dogs being loving companions, and the bravest of all animals determinedly winning their way through to our hearts.

Dogs and children

For a child, the benefits of having a dog at home are considerable and well researched. Generally, adding a puppy to the family in the preschool years helps children to develop their own confidence and acquire a sense of responsibility. As puppies are generally very social, saying big happy hellos to everyone they meet, the child's own social experiences and skill levels are also quickly developed.

Paediatrician, Jennifer Mullally. M.D., from Sanford Health, writes:

'Taking care of another living being teaches humanity and responsibility which we can all benefit from.'

The Human Animal Bond Research Institute (HABRI) has supported a variety of studies into the

emotional benefits for children of family dog ownership, and a trawl of the internet can produce many more. Among these benefits are engaging in other social interactions, sharing things, not engaging in anti-social activities, and generally being happier and less anxious.

A study by the Telethon Kids Institute and the University of Western Australia (UWA) reinforces some of these findings by demonstrating that kids with dogs get more exercise, sleep better and, of course, have less screen time.

But puppies will not bring an instantaneous benefit to any household. Proper care and training is required, and the results and accompanying joy are incremental.

But do we really need studies to tell us this? Studies are, of course, useful but for dog lovers studies simply 'prove' what to them is obvious. Perhaps it's time the rest of the world caught up!

The much-loved children's picture book *Cookie* captures the impact a dog can have on a family. Written in the dog's voice, it shows how a new puppy can ease a child's depression: 'Girl tried to play. But she was too sad. So, we cuddled instead ...I helped so much Girl got happier. And everyone is happier when girl is happier. Especially me.'

‘There are those that believe dogs are incapable of knowing right from wrong and that they respond only to orders and to brainwashing forms of behaviour but, if this were so, a dog would be a very boring animal.’

— *Katharine Tottenham*

Dog years

We have always wanted to equate dog years to human years. This gets complicated due to variation within breeds; however, the American Veterinary Medical Association has a helpful breakdown suggesting that the first year of an average dog's life is equivalent to fifteen human years. The next year for the dog equates to nine more human years; thereafter, each dog year is equivalent to four human years. For example, a four-year-old dog would be equivalent to a 32-year-old human.

Small dogs, when properly cared for, can normally live up to sixteen years and larger breeds up to fourteen years. In addition to variations by breed, a dog's longevity can, just like a human's, be profoundly influenced by their health and care. For example, a recent study showed that overweight Labrador Retrievers live two years less than their fitter counterparts.

While it can be hard to verify claims to be the 'oldest' dog, Bobi, a purebred Portuguese Rafeiro do Alentjo, is believed to have lived to be 31 years old. Bobi shared his home with his owner Costa and four cats in Conqueiros, in Portugal's Leiria district. Bobi never had any special dog food and just ate what everyone else in the family did. Like them, Bobi enjoyed plenty of love and fresh air and Bobi had never been on a leash. He was popular as well, with over 100 people attending his final birthday party!

Loyalty

Fiction is full of stories celebrating a dog's loyalty. Perhaps the most famous story involves Odysseus from Homer's *Odyssey* reuniting momentarily with his dog, Argos, who died just after welcoming him home to Ithaca after a twenty-year wait. The important twist in this story is that Argos realized his greeting needed to be discreet as public recognition would put Odysseus at risk of prematurely shedding his disguise.

A dog's real-life loyalty to its owner is often cited as one of its most-loved characteristics. There are many heartbreaking stories of a dog's loyalty being demonstrated long after the owner's death. Famous dogs like Fido and Hachikō, who kept multiyear vigils at their past meeting places with their long-dead owners, are often cited. Many dog owners can relate stories of their dogs who returned home over incredible distances or stood by their master awaiting his rescue or did everything possible to keep the household toddler safe.

Yes, dogs are pack animals and loyalty to the pack is crucial to survival. Yet there is clearly more to a dog's loyalty than instinct. It's not hard to imagine that a dog's behaviour towards its human is the purest example of unconditional love, as demonstrated in the following story about Boudica, a Great Pyrenees.

The Great Pyrenees is perhaps one of the most regal and independent-thinking of breeds. The Farmer-ish website has this not untypical story about Boudica's owner going for a walk without her and being barked at by a labrador.

'I heard this ferocious almost hysterical bark from Boudica. It was like her worst fears had been realized. There I was, her helpless human, out in the world with another dog surely about to attack me and she was not with me! She was beside herself.' Boudica's owner made sure that he was never barked at again where she could hear it.

'Dogs come into our lives to teach us about love and loyalty. They depart to teach us about loss. A new dog never replaces an old dog, it merely expands the heart. If you have loved many dogs your heart is very big.'

— Erica Jong

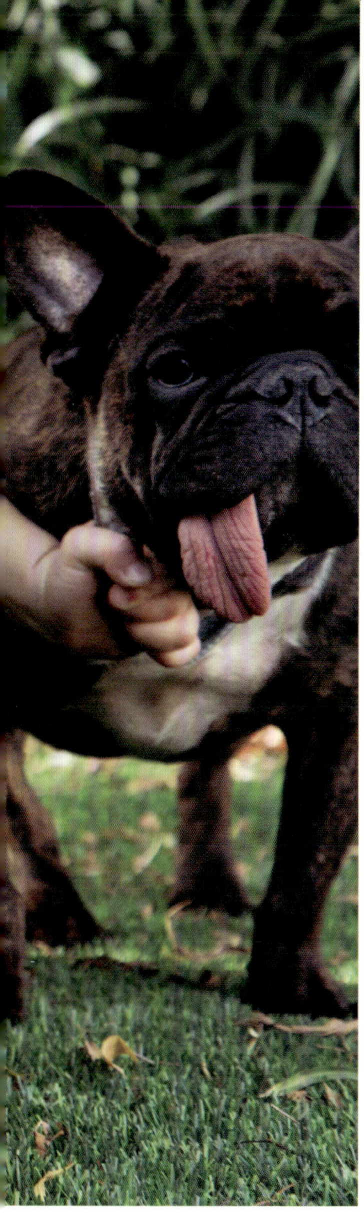

Affection

Because dogs can often be loud and boisterous, there is a risk you may not see just how much affection they are showing you.

When your dog leans into you, it's an obvious sign of affection and trust. They can lean into you in many circumstances, including when they are feeling insecure and they are trusting you to look after them. Borrowing your clothes to have your scent near them or seeking to share their favourite toy with you are other signs of love and affection. So too is eye contact and tail wagging, both of which can release the attachment- and trust-building hormone oxytocin. Watch what your dog's eyebrows are doing — lifting them is a sign of affection as well.

When you come home and your dog zips around the room and spins around in circles, they are showing you their love and excitement about your return. Licking you is also an obvious sign of affection — unless you have just been eating something particularly tasty!

Dogs at the vet

The veterinary industry suggests that you should budget around US$400 or equivalent per month for vet bills. This allows for the occasional emergency. There is a series of inoculations recommended between six and eighteen weeks old and a yearly booster. There are also regular health checks, a worming schedule plus whatever treatments are needed after injuries and accidents. It's no surprise that pet insurance seems to be an ever-growing industry. The first dog to ever receive insurance was in Sweden in the early 1920s, and some pet policies were issued in Britain not long after the Second World War, but it wasn't until the 1980s that USA and Canadian pet insurance became properly established. It has since spread across much of the world.

Dogs will often become anxious when taken to the vet and if this, in turn, makes you anxious and your dog senses that, the whole event can become difficult from the outset. Painful memories, distressing smells, and signals from other animals can all be difficult to process. The attitude and approach of your vet and their staff can make a substantial difference.

For vets — who must make a living — dealing with complicated issues with pet dogs that have uninsured and financially unprepared owners can be highly stressful. The internet has many stories of generous strangers helping out, but that seems like a high-risk strategy. Better to recognize that keeping a dog does require ready cash and a reserve fund or insurance. Some vets offer the occasional subsidized or free service, so if you cannot have insurance, it would be wise to research these options before you might need them.

‘Don’t accept your dog’s admiration as conclusive evidence that you are wonderful.’

— Ann Landers

‘The capacity for love that makes dogs such rewarding companions has a flip side: they find it difficult to cope without us. Since we humans have programmed this vulnerability, it’s our responsibility to ensure that our dogs do not suffer as a result.’

— *John Bradshaw*

‘Happiness is a warm puppy.’

— *Charles M. Schulz*

Dogs and your child's health

With hundreds of millions of households keeping dogs, it's not surprising that there are many scientific research projects about the health benefits or otherwise that a dog can bring to your children.

Authoritative veterinary medical news site, dvm360, reported on two studies presented at the American College of Allergy, Asthma and Immunology (ACAAI). These showed that a baby born in a home where there was a dog present during the pregnancy receives protection from allergic eczema, although the protective effect goes down by age ten. The studies also showed dogs may provide a protective effect against asthma, even in children allergic to dogs.

‘Dogs have a way of finding the people who need them and filling an emptiness we didn’t even know we had.’

— Thom Jones

Growth rate of dogs

In around six months, a small puppy is likely to have reached three-quarters of its full size. By the end of its first year, it will be full sized. Big dogs take longer, reaching about half their full size within their fifth month, while very big dogs can take up to eighteen months to reach their full size.

Even within breeds dogs can have quite different sizes and it's sometimes hard to predict just how big a dog will become. Diet, gender and just the right amount of exercise have an enormous influence. Often, the larger the puppy's paws, the bigger the dog will be, but some small dogs do have large paws. Look at the legs as well: the longer and sturdier they appear, the greater the chance that the puppy will grow into a large or at least a medium-sized dog. Smaller and thinner legs can conversely indicate that the puppy will become a small dog. If you know the puppy's pedigree, its relatives — especially parents and grandparents — will provide a good indication of future size.

Sea dogs

Many dogs just love being in and on water and make great companions for sailors. Often, the space aboard a ship is limited, so sailing with a small dog can provide easy undemanding company.

The US Navy has kept dogs, and not just as mascots, for over 150 years. Dogs at sea provide great morale boosters to sailors far away from home. They are something everyone aboard can care for and discuss.

Dog breeds like Terriers can deal with rats, others can provide protective company on strange shores, and others are trained and bred for a variety of tasks. The Labrador's webbed paws help it to retrieve fish and fishing nets, while Portuguese Water Dogs can herd fish into nets and deliver ship-to-ship messages.

'The greatest pleasure of a dog is that you may make a fool of yourself with him, and not only will he not scold you, but he will make a fool of himself too.'

— Samuel Butler

Bringing a dog on a first date

The internet is awash with questions and advice as to whether or not to bring a dog on the first date. The consensus seems to be that it is not a great idea, and if each person brings a dog, that can be fraught with difficulty. Yet, with some planning, having dogs on a date can be a big success.

Pets provide a shared safe subject to talk about and seeing how 'the date' deals with a dog can be very revealing. Are they kind and attentive? Is their dog a designer breed and little more than a status symbol? Is the dog happy, curious and secure ... or clinging and anxious?

If two strange dogs are together, seeing how they get along can provide useful information for any future romantic intentions. Like people, dogs need time to get used to one another, and how secure the date's dog is might just tell you something about the owner.

Dogs do have an impact on human relationships and can bring out the best in people. But if your date is jealous of the time and energy you spend with your dog, that can tell you something too.

‘Everyone thinks they have the best dog. And none of them are wrong.’

— W.R. Purche

Reading to dogs

Encouraging children to read can sometimes be difficult. A child might also be shy about reading aloud when there are lots of other people around. However, therapy dogs have been employed in schools for a while, and Educational Support Dogs are now in high demand.

Psychology Today reports that 'Reading out loud to a dog improves reading comprehension even more than reading to an adult.' ABC News reported that a University of California study showed that, over a ten-week program, children who read out loud to their dog improved their reading skills by 12 per cent over those who didn't.

Children don't seem to mind reading to dogs. Dogs are of course great listeners, and won't comment on reading pace or hesitations. The child may well feel highly motivated to entertain their best friend as well as possible. Better still, the dog doesn't laugh when mistakes are made, so the child's confidence can quickly build, in turn potentially cultivating a love of reading.

‘A dog will teach you unconditional love. If you can have that in your life, things won’t be too bad.’

— *Robert Wagner*

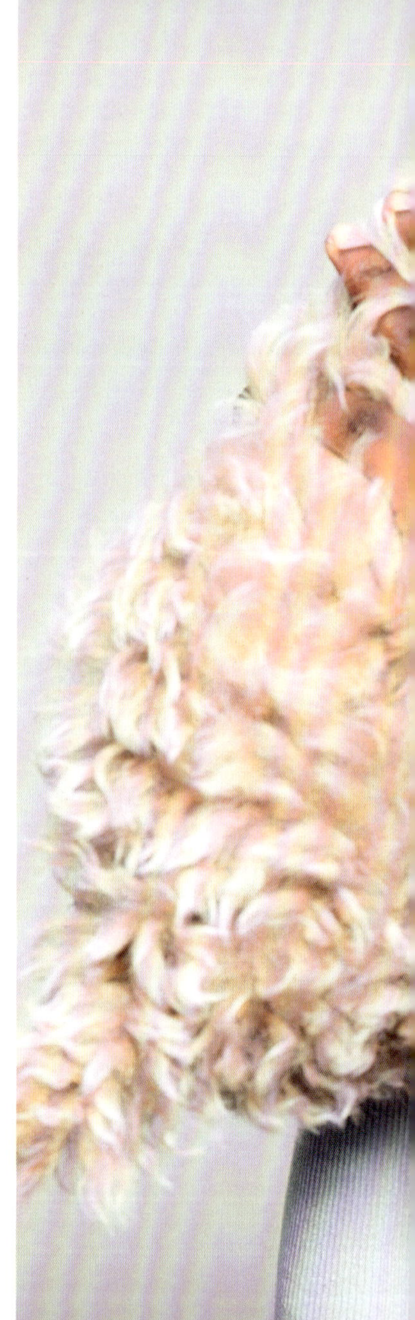

Dogs keep us fit

The Mayo Clinic reports that 'dogs force us to get up and move for routine and regular walks. A research study found that dog owners more likely report regular physical activity patterns, a healthy diet and ideal blood sugar levels compared to those who do not own dogs.'

The American Heart Association lists '16 science-backed reasons adopting a dog could be good for your heart.' These include generally increased physical activity, and the happiness and concurrent decline in blood pressure caused by petting and enjoying a dog. Dog owners' risk of contracting diabetes or having a heart attack is about 30 per cent lower than non-dog owners, and the benefit of a supportive companion and the social contact they attract enhances every owner's life. In short, with a dog, you are going to live with less stress, stay healthier and enjoy life more!

Exercise with dogs need not be confined to walking. Dogs make great companions for cyclists; many make excellent swimming buddies; and if you enjoy chasing each other, your dog can really help you become strong and fit. Dogs, of course, always need exercise and that means you are obliged to get outside and move in most weather conditions even if you would otherwise choose to stay indoors.

The United Kingdom's Barking Mad website lists key ways dogs and owners benefit from daily walks including strengthening the relationship between the dog and human, keeping weight in check, preventing loneliness — for both parties — and increasing physical and mental health.

‘The world would be a nicer place if everyone had the ability to love as unconditionally as a dog.’

— M.K. Clinton

HO! HO! HO!
OH! WHAT
HO! HO!

Dogs and seniors

Dogs are not a solution to the difficulties of old age and declining health; however, when it's possible to keep a dog, major health risk factors of ageing are significantly decreased.

One of this century's prevailing epidemics is the blight of loneliness, and the older we are the more likely we are to live alone. The Human Animal Bond Research Institute reports that an analysis of nearly 150 long-term studies, involving around 300,000 people, showed people with some meaningful form of consistent social contact have a 50 per cent greater chance of survival than those without.

There's no doubt that dog ownership increases social contact and the owner's sense of security. Dr Christian from the University of Western Australia was reported in *The Daily Telegraph* as saying 'dog owners are not only more physically active on more days of the week but the presence of dogs has neighbours feeling the area is more secure.' An Australian study found that '42 per cent of the people said that they had met someone through their pet that they could turn to.'

Having a dog regularly in your life brings other health benefits. Interacting with a pet dog can release oxytocin and dopamine, which help you feel good. Conversely, petting a dog lowers stress-related cortisol. People who walk their dogs also have lower obesity rates than people who do not exercise, and an additional benefit is the reduction in the risk of cardiovascular disease.

Even if you are unfortunate enough to have had a heart attack, Swedish research has found that heart attack patients living alone with a dog are 33 per cent less likely to die than if they lived completely alone.

Dogs in offices

'You might get your worker back in the office if you let them bring their dog.'

— *Fortune*

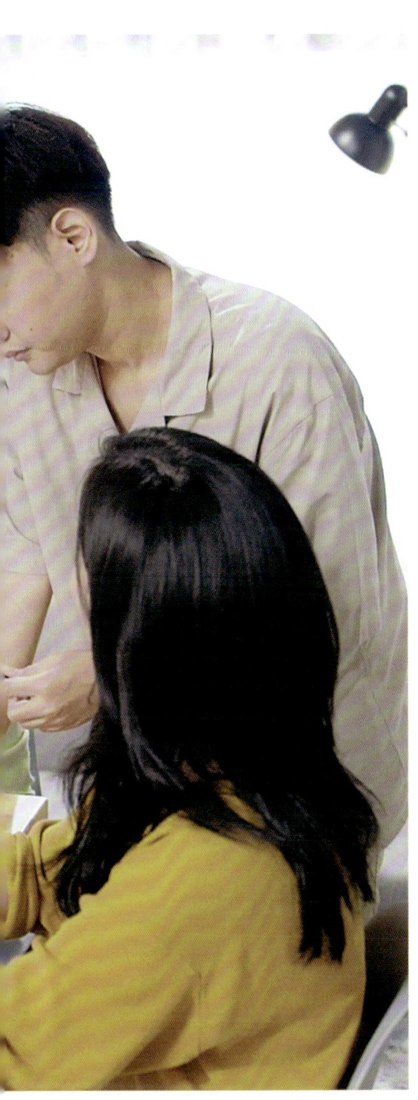

Since Covid made hybrid working and full-time work-from-home a regular part of workers' lives, dogs and humans have benefitted from far more of each other's company than the '9 to 5' going-to-work regime allowed. *The Guardian* newspaper writes that 'Allowing employees to bring their pets to work could be a powerful way to entice those wary workers out of their homes and back to the office.'

Everyone's office is different. The United Kingdom's Get Set Pet website relays that 'studies have shown that people who work with dogs are more likely to take breaks and move around during the day, this can lead to better focus and concentration. And since breaks are essential for productivity having a dog in the office can help you get more done.'

Increasingly, big companies like Amazon and Google are conditionally happy for employees to bring their dogs to work. Tokyo's Fujitsu started experimenting with dogs at work and the trend accelerated around the world as a way to get people back to the office after the Covid work-from-home era. It's a trend that shows no sign of slowing down.

Where to pet a dog

It is, of course, important to pet your dog — and most dogs need and love this — but doing it the right way is vital.

There is lots of free advice about how to pet a dog. Daily Paws makes it clear that the most important thing is to make sure you have permission to do so: 'Pet for a few seconds then pause,' giving the dog a chance to indicate whether or not further attention is wanted. Petsmont, an organic pet products company, cautions 'to not make direct eye contact. Eye contact with humans is something all dogs actually hate, but not many people are aware of this.'

Other advice suggests that you should be gentle, pet, not pat, and keep clear of the paws and the muzzle. Avoid the top of the head, and at first just pet neutral areas such as under the chin. The more a dog knows and trusts you, the more areas they will want you to pet them on. Until then be very cautious and, in all cases, very respectful of the dog's needs and space.

What's the best dog breed to keep you safe?

Assuming that you don't live in an unusually dangerous environment and that you take comprehensive care of your dog, these breeds consistently make it to the top of lists of the best dogs to have for your safety if you live alone.

German Shepherds are highly intelligent, loyal dogs who graduated from sheep herding to police work during the First World War. You can now find them involved in many human endeavours, from assisting uniformed forces to being guard dogs. Most importantly, they are family friendly. However, being very intelligent, they require significant time from their owners, and intellectual as well as physical challenges.

Doberman Pinschers, also of German origin, are loyal and protective and are now one of the world's most popular breeds. They are known to sometimes bond with just one person, but when socialized properly, they can make a marvellous family dog.

Rottweilers are courageous, loyal and intelligent dogs that can become much-loved family pets, often with a tendency to show a great deal of affection. Like all big dogs, Rottweilers require a lot of time, exercise and training.

The Boxer is a less intense breed than the others but it is still very capable of protecting you and your family. Boxers are also playful and love children.

‘Blessed is the person who has earned the love of a Boxer.’

— *Woopooch Press*

Doberman Pinscher

In the 1880s, in Thuringia, Germany, Karl Friedrich Louis Dobermann was a nightwatchman at a dog pound and, during the day, a tax collector. The story goes that he sought to breed a protective companion from the dogs available in the pound. Eventually, what we recognize today as the Doberman emerged. There are several variations, including a chocolate-brown one, but they are all protective, friendly, full of energy, and great companions.

Best breeds for snuggles

According to Spruce Pets' website, the best dog breeds for cuddling include the **Golden Retriever**. An almost universal family favourite, this breed is marvellous with children. They are also intelligent and easy to train. The Golden Retriever's capacity for friendship is legendary, not just with humans, and the internet is awash with stories about Golden Retriever friendships with other animals, including a dolphin.

America's most popular breed, the **Labrador**, has similar characteristics to the Golden Retriever but is both more cautious around strangers and a little bit more energetic. This arguably makes them better guard dogs. However, both breeds are full of love and affection and a delight in any household. Labradors have a thick tail, webbed feet, and a watertight coat that makes them love jumping in the sea — actually any water they can find. Including goldfish ponds.

The **King Charles Spaniel** is a great breed for cuddling too. They can be affectionate with almost everyone and also get along well with other dogs. One of the most adaptable of the more cuddle-oriented dogs, the King Charles is equally happy actively playing with a four year old or sitting quietly with a 94 year old. The American and English King Charles Spaniels are different breeds but share most of the same characteristics. Not always the most intellectually gifted of breeds, they have been known to chase anything that moves. Including cars.

The **Pomeranian** is a cute, noisy and, when not getting enough attention, bossy little dog, but mostly they are affectionate and love being always with you as a fellow pack member. Pomeranians have been described as having the heart of a lion and the attitude of a Great Dane. A Pomeranian will often be the dog that starts a barking match or street squabble, but can quickly transform into an irresistible ball of fluff that considers your lap to be their personal property.

There are very few dogs who don't like being close to their humans on a regular basis, and the more your dog trusts you, the more affectionate they are likely to be. Developing this trust depends to some extent on how you raise them. As with all aspects of training, taking your time and being consistent will make all the difference.

After you have built a loving, trusting, affectionate bond with your dog, it's worth keeping an eye open for any changes in behaviour. When the occasional lick becomes an incessant habit, or requests for strokes suddenly increase or diminish, something will have changed for your dog. It's your job to deduce what that is. A dog's need for giving and receiving affection is a reliable window into what is going on for it. There is always a reason behind any sudden change.

Corgi: big dog, small legs

The Pembroke Welsh Corgi is the size of a big lap dog but has an attitude similar to that of many working dogs. They need to be kept active, as their short stature allows, and intellectually stimulated. They were bred to move cattle and are known to be quite fearless. This together with their very big-dog-sized bark makes them effective watch-dogs. They are also playful and endlessly loyal to whoever they consider is in their pack.

Her Royal Majesty Queen Elizabeth had more than 30 of these Corgis in her lifetime and referred to them as family members. The two that survived the Queen, Sandy and Muick, went on to thrive in the Duchess of York's care.

How long have dogs been our best friends?

Dogs have been with us for thousands of years, with a variety of cultures showing them performing caring and supportive roles for humans.

Aztec and Mayan cultures believed dogs to be messengers between the world of the living and the dead. Ancient Egyptians held similar beliefs, and dogs were known to be hard at work with the Egyptians at least 8000 years ago. Lord Dattatreya, a major Hindu deity, is often depicted with four dogs, representing the states of the world. China's Han Dynasty's burial sites often contain dog figures. Ancient imperial China gave Pekingese special treatment in the Forbidden City. Dogs were also kept by the Ancient Romans and Greeks.

Jack Russell terrier

The Jack Russell, when properly trained and socialized, is a happy, energetic, assertive and sometimes stubborn dog.

Jack Russells were first bred in England to be fox hunters and have since been used to deal with any ground-based prey. A chaplain in the First World War used his dog to rid trenches of rats. Jack Russells can even be found aboard ships, where their balance and agility make them ideal travellers and rodent killers.

The Jack Russell's bouncy nature is irresistible to just about everyone. Some owners send their Jack Russell into teenagers' bedrooms to get the kids up for school. And if they ever lose a tennis ball, the Jack Russell is the likely finder.

A Jack Russell's sense of smell sees them employed sniffing for drugs in airports and seeking out bombs wherever needed. Patron, a Jack Rusell terrier, has been credited by Ukrainian officials for sniffing out and thereby neutralizing around 90 explosive devices.

‘Dogs are our link to paradise. They don’t know evil or jealousy or discontent. To sit with a dog on a hillside on a glorious afternoon is to be back in Eden, where doing nothing was not boring — it was peace.’

— *Milan Kundera*

Dogs to the rescue

From mountains to the sea, from being lost in forests, sinking with a shipwreck, being trapped in fallen buildings, or being overrun by an avalanche, if you are lucky there will be a dog looking for you. However, dogs cannot be experts in all conditions and terrains, so there is increasing specialization.

Avalanche dogs

In many countries, avalanche rescue dog work has been handled by police dogs. However, the demands on general police resources has seen the need for specialized snow-focused dog teams grow, and the Search and Rescue Dogs Avalanche NZ organization (SARDA) is a good example of this. New Zealand has ski operations in both its main islands and there are now seventeen fully trained avalanche rescue dogs throughout the country.

SARDA's National Coordinator, Karyn Robertson, explains that fast, skilled dogs, with their vastly superior sense of smell to humans, can quickly find a body covered by snow. Speed is of the essence in an avalanche, and when dogs work in pairs a lot of ground can be rapidly covered. Often dogs are sited at ski centres as experts stress the need to deploy dogs rapidly before the human rescuers. 'We have just twenty minutes to find you — thereafter it's probably too late.'

It can take over two years for the dogs to be fully trained. Typically, they are Labrador Retrievers in New Zealand, whose big feet can help propel them across the snow rather than sink into it. German Shepherds and Border Collies are also trained; elsewhere in the world you may still find the

legendary brandy-toting Saint Bernard.

Karyn Robertson's team of volunteer handlers are generally involved, in one way or another, with snow in their work lives and they bring this expertise to the dogs' training. As well as being primed and ready for front-line action on the ski fields, New Zealand's avalanche dogs are put to work checking avalanche sites in the back country to ensure they have not claimed any lives. The avalanche dogs' resources are inter-operable with those of the New Zealand Police force.

Water rescue dogs

Labradors, Golden Retrievers and Portuguese Water Dogs are great swimmers and rescue dogs. However, the most powerful is the Newfoundland. The Newfoundland originated in Canada as a fisherman's working dog. They are very strong, have double water-resistant coats and webbed feet, and you will find them on duty throughout the world.

Most of Italy's 300 coast guard dogs are Newfoundlands.

Ferruccio Pilenga was inspired to start the Italian School for Lifeguard Dogs by a story, shared on the school's website, which starts with a wave crashing onto the deck of an ancient sailing ship: 'To the dismay of those onboard a man washed overboard. Everybody felt helpless. Suddenly a black shape leapt into the freezing water and surging waves, catching the man and pulling him back to the boat, saving his life. The hero answered to the name of his land of origin, Terranova [Newfoundland].'

Tracking dogs

Wherever you are lost on land, a search and rescue dog can track you down, even picking up a scent trail that's several days old. These dogs have the skills to find you if you are unable to make a sound or even if you don't want to be found! Bloodhounds are the most famous trackers, but often Golden and Labrador Retrievers and German Shepherd dogs are trained for tracking. Rescue dogs can work with minimal light and be in action long before the two-legged team members, and the dog's tenacity, especially a Bloodhound's, makes them a vital part of many police forces and rescue organizations around the world.

The interplay of trust and communication between the handler and the tracking dog is the currency that makes all successful tracking and rescues possible. Training for all kinds of rescue and tracking work is a demanding process for both the dog and the trainer. Very often there are certification levels to achieve as well as a battery of other tests. Uniformed forces and rescue associations, many of which rely on volunteers, know that their purpose is to save lives, so training is necessarily comprehensive.

Explosive detector dogs

A Princeton University paper on 'Technology Against Terrorism' states that 'There is no mechanical device that is as accurate, fast, sensitive, mobile, flexible and durable as a well-trained dog handler team.'

As security protocols get ever tighter, the demand for trained explosive detector dogs continues to rise. Dogs suited to this work include the always useful Golden and Labrador Retrievers, Vizslas and German Wire- and Short-Haired Pointers.

A close cousin to the Weimaraner, the Vizsla has always hunted alongside mankind. They are bright, energetic, loyal, and keen to please, so if trained to find explosives, they will seek to please their trainer by finding them.

The German Short-Haired Pointer is probably a little brighter and even more eager to please than its Wire-Haired cousin, but a little less family oriented. Both make excellent detector dogs.

'If you don't own a dog, at least one, there may not necessarily be anything wrong with you, but there may be something wrong with your life.'

— *Roger Caras*

Jacobson's organ

Dogs' sniffing ability is put to use all over the world with many different kinds of dogs at work, including Beagles, Labradors, German Shepherds, Bloodhounds and English Springer Spaniels.

Dogs interpret the world through smell. Helping them do this is a special device called Jacobson's organ; it is situated in the nasal cavity and opens up into the back of the mouth and its nerve system flowing directly into the brain. This organ picks up odours that we find undetectable. Keep an eye on your dog when the nostrils flare: the super-smelling ability is in action, putting 300 million olfactory receptors to work (as a comparison, humans only have around 6 million receptors).

Dogs, especially those with long noses, can sniff out diseases, smell when you are stressed, and find buried earthquake victims.

Deans Services, a Florida-based lawn, termite and pest-control business, provides the services of their Beagles, Scratch and Emily, who achieve a 94 per cent accuracy rating for detecting termites. This is much more than humans can do alone and can help prevent termite damage before it becomes serious.

Fire rescue services have specially trained arson dogs that are taught to sniff out any accelerants such as diesel fuel or lighter fluid that might have been used to assist a fire. During training, the dogs are imprinted on specific odours, and they can continue identifying these for around eight working years. We also know that dogs can detect pathogens and viruses, and Alabama's Auburn University has a specialized team at their Canine Performance Sciences program working on developing specific canine detection abilities.

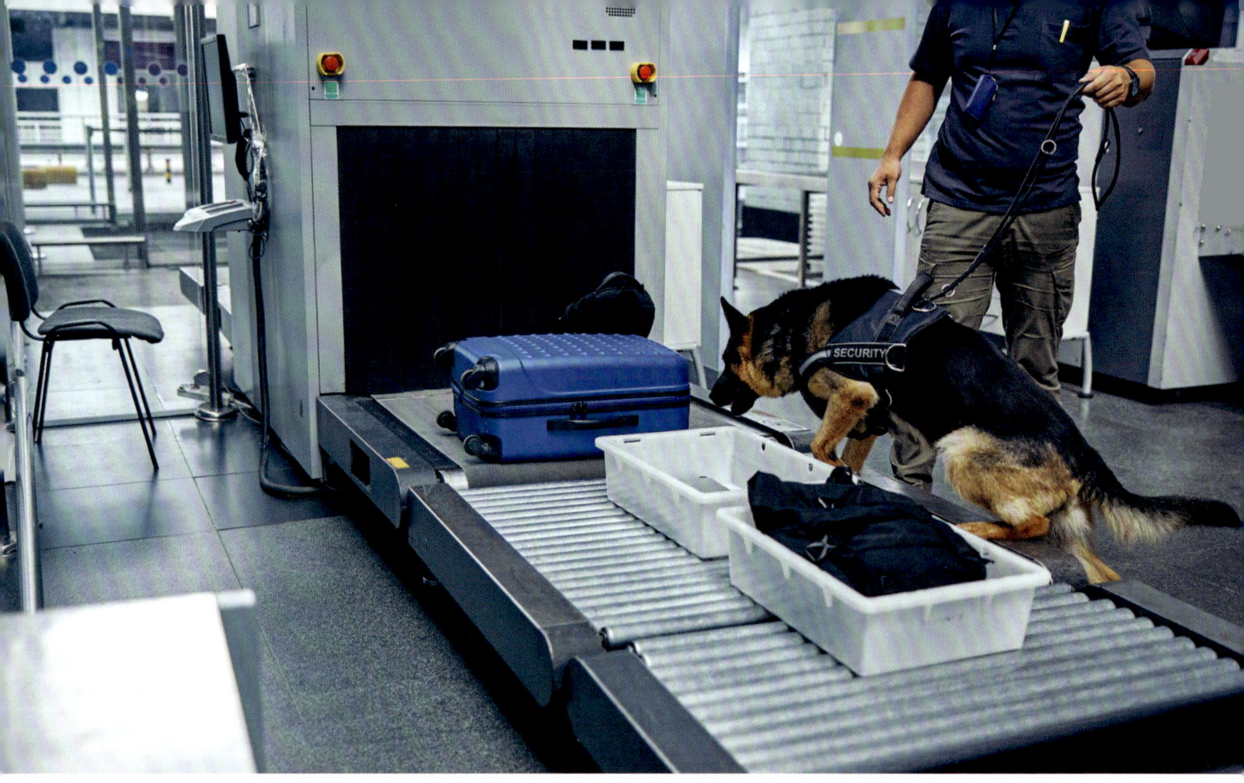

Getting to work as a detector dog requires very high standards of stamina and discipline, in addition to sensitive smell; obedience and training processes eliminate a lot of dogs. For example, the Canadian Border Services Agency Detector Dog Service program accepts, after evaluation, only one in ten applicants.

The Australian Border Force has its own breeding process, managing the fostering of puppies for the first year. Dogs and trainers must both complete demanding courses, with the dogs being trained to find currency, tobacco, illicit drugs, firearms and explosives. Australia, like New Zealand, is necessarily rigorous in protecting the nation from unwanted social, agricultural or environmentally damaging products and pests. In both nations, the role of detector dogs is vitally important.

Across the world, companies like NZ Detector Dogs also offer the private services of trained detector dogs for drug searches across a variety of industries. In Britain and elsewhere, you can find companies offering courses on scent-training for dogs and handlers. Some courses can even be done online. One way or another, we are exploring the potential for making good use of dogs' olfactory sensitivity.

‘Before you get a dog you can’t quite imagine what living with one might be like; afterward you can’t imagine living any other way.’

— *Caroline Knapp*

Statue to loyalty

There are not many things that most people in the world can agree about, but the love of dogs is one of them. We are impressed by, grateful for, and indeed dependent upon their many skills, but if you own a dog, it's mostly the simplest of things that matter.

If your family leaves the home during the day, you will know that your dog is sad to see you go. You would have seen the unattributed quote 'happiness is coming home knowing that your dog awaits you.'

Apart from an enthusiastic lovable greeting, what do we look forward to with our dogs? The unconditional love? The adoration? The often sweet nature? The warmth and the fun? The companionship and the joy? Or all of the above at differing times? Or even all at the same time? For some, merely keeping a dog creates a valuable and almost completely unavoidable exercise regime. After all, who, if they are truly alive, would rather watch television than play with a dog? Who can truly resist a dog's affection or not enjoy their silliness? But in the end, perhaps it is a dog's loyalty to their owners that is most impressive.

There is the story of a statue in the city of Tolyatti on the Volga River. Two people were killed in a car crash but their German Shepherd, named Kostya, was unscathed. His people were taken away but for seven years Kostya came back to look for them at the crash site. The local people looked after him as well as they could, and after his death erected a larger-than-life-size statue for him called 'Loyalty.' Nowadays, newlywed couples rub the statue's nose to safe-guard their loyalty to each other.

Dalmatians

The British Dalmatian Club describes the breed as 'a carriage dog of good demeanour capable of great endurance and a fair turn of speed.' The club describes their temperament as 'outgoing and friendly, not shy or hesitant, free from nervousness and aggression.'

As a carriage dog, Dalmatians used to travel on either side of the vehicle and sometimes under the axle. They cleared the road of stray dogs and kept up with and protected the horses from other risks and impediments. Noblemen and gypsies alike valued these exceptional animals. "

The Dalmatian club in Victoria, Australia, writes, 'Elegance and humour are the hallmarks of the breed. He is a fun-loving natural clown. His "smile" is often taken for a snarl, unless one spots his furiously wagging tail.'

In North America, Dalmatians are closely associated with fire services; many of them have Dalmatians as mascots in recognition of the breed's previous service accompanying and clearing the way for horse-drawn fire trucks.

50 St
ENGINE
F.D.N.Y.
343
9-11-01
FIRE FAMILY TRANSPORT
FOUNDATION
SEPT. 11, 2001
343
FDNY

The naming of dog breeds

Though many breed names are straightforward and easy to understand, some are misleading and others confusing. Dog names are, of course, part of our own complex and long history.

Nobody is clear where Dalmatians came from, though perhaps they did just come from the Adriatic coastal region of Dalmatia, Croatia. But we are clear that, despite its name, the Australian Shepherd came from the United States. Or did it? Purina's website states, 'The Australian Shepherd derived his name from his association with the Basque Shepherd dogs that came to the US from Australia in the 1800s.'

Beagles sounds almost exactly nothing akin to the trumpet-like instrument, the bugle, but it's how the breed is rumoured to have gained its name, or perhaps it's from the French word *begueule*, meaning 'gaped throat.'

Karl Friedrich Louis Dobermann, the tax collector, gave his name to the breed he developed. Shih Tzu translates to 'little lion' and Schnauzer translates to 'snout.'

Bloodhounds are supposedly so named, not for the ability to track humans, but because they have a pure-bred nobility to them. Great Danes are almost certainly not Danish. Pit Bulls and Bull Dogs are probably named after violent forms of 'entertainment.' Saint Bernards are named from whence they came, likewise the Rottweiler. Poodles found their name from the German word for 'puddle.' Dachshund is, in the German language, a badger dog.

There is some argument about how Boxers got their name. Some people saying that they used to control cattle in German slaughterhouses, known as *boxls*. Others say that the way the

breed stands up and plays with its front paws is akin to the way human boxers move. Bichon Frisé is derived from the French for 'curly haired small dog.'

Cavalier King Charles comes from Charles II. His father, a supporter of Cavaliers during the war, was executed by the opposition Roundheads. When installed on the throne, Charles II added the 'Cavalier' to this spaniel's breed name.

Chihuahuas are named after the Mexican state bordering the USA, where the breed supposedly originated.

‘We live in a fragmented and disconnected culture. Politics are ugly, religion is struggling, technology is stressful, and the economy is unfortunate. What’s one thing that we have in our lives that we can depend on? A dog loving us unconditionally, every day, very faithfully.’

— *Jon Katz*

Dogs in film and literature

The Canadian writer Leon Rooke used 'Shakespeare's pet dog Hooker' to tell the tale of the Bard's early years. Shakespeare himself could have little use for dogs, as his stages were in loud, often bawdy, round theatres, so the only well-known on-stage canine reference is to Crab in *The Two Gentlemen of Verona*, a comedy written around 1590. Lance, one of two servants in the play, uses Crab as a foil for his quick-witted comedic lines. From Act 2 scene IV:

'Ask my dog. If he says "Ay" it will. If he says "No" it will. If he shakes his tail and say nothing it will.'

Lassie

Probably the best known TV and film dog character is Lassie. Lassie's stories concern a Baltimore family moving to rural Virginia and adopting a Collie who becomes the son's amazing companion. The TV series ran for around seventeen years and showed just how good canine and human relationships can be.

Lady and the Tramp

When the animated Walt Disney movie *Lady and the Tramp* was released in 1955, the critics weren't sure about it, but the public was, and there have been remakes and reissues of this much-loved classic ever since. In 2023, the Library of Congress recognized it as being of great importance and selected it for preservation in the National Film Registry. The sweet love story between the rough mutt and upscale Cocker Spaniel has now entertained generations.

Rin Tin Tin

In a hastily deserted German trench in war-torn First World War France, Lee Duncan, a soldier from California, found a staring German Shepherd with five tiny and struggling puppies. Lee took Rin Tin Tin and his sister home and he proved to be exceptionally trainable and athletic. Warner Bros., then a tiny and emerging studio, invested heavily in him and made 26 silent Western-style adventures complete with Cavalry troops, thieves and heroes. The last one was released in 1930. Rin Tin Tin died, still an active performer, in 1932.

Rin Tin Tin's friendship with a boy enriched Warner Bros., built the popularity of German Shepherds, and warmed the hearts of generations of children of all ages. Rin Tin Tin's descendants continued playing the role throughout the 1950s. Susan Orlean, a best-selling author, has written a book about Rin Tin Tin and says, 'This was not just a story about a dog or even the many dogs that make up the Rin Tin Tin family; this is the story of a beloved icon who has played a role in decades of American popular culture.'

Toto

Toto was the Cairn Terrier in *The Wizard of Oz*, first shown in 1939. Toto's pre-movie name was Terry and he

was raised by Carl Spitz, who ran a dog-training school and was involved in other dog-oriented movies such as *The Daring Dobermans* and *Mean Dog Blues*. Mischievous and playful, Toto even exposed the wizard. Toto was reputedly the highest-paid actor in the movie!

Old Yeller

Set in a post-Civil War Texas ranch, this celebrated 1957 movie features a runaway dog that saves a young boy from a bear attack and then becomes a close family member. Old Yeller has many adventures, but they conclude with his successfully fighting off a wolf but being bitten in the process. There was a rabies scare at the time and Old Yeller had to be put down to protect him and everyone else from rabies. This ending, with its lesson about the need to make tough decisions, did not hurt *Old Yeller*'s popularity.

Hooch

Beethoven, Scooby Doo, all 101 Dalmatians, Bolt, Wishbone, Hooch, Marley, Bruiser and the team of *PAW Patrol* are just a few of the many dog characters to have blessed our screens. Real-life dogs are generally trained by film-industry experts who use clickers to control their dogs. Quality actors such as Tom Hanks invest the time and energy necessary to get to know their dog counterparts and create a genuine connection, so it both looks and feels real for the viewers. Getting to know the French Mastiff in *Turner & Hooch* took Hanks weeks.

For hundreds of years dogs have been used to highlight the human condition's strengths and weaknesses. Only comparatively recently have dogs been given a generally positive light. Old phrases such as 'going to the dogs' and even the word 'doggerel' just have a negative connotation. Similarly, most of the references in the Bible to dogs are far from complimentary; for example, 'Watch out for those dogs, those evildoers, those mutilators of the flesh' and 'Dogs surround me, a pack of villains encircles me.'

Known as the 'people's author,' Charles Dickens (1812–1870) was one of the first truly popular writers dealing with social issues. Dickens was writing at a time when humans were increasingly viewing dogs as companions, and kept several himself. Dickens used dogs to throw light on human tendencies and *Oliver Twist*'s Bullseye, which belonged to the violent Bill Sikes, had 'faults of temper in common with his owner and

labouring, perhaps at this moment, under a powerful sense of injury made no more ado but at once fixed his teeth into one of the half boots.' While Dicken's dog character Jip, who belonged to Copperfield's wife Dora, is a classical spoilt lap dog spaniel, dominating his mistress who doted upon him.

Cerberus, the hound of Hades in Greek mythology, has been credited with having many heads (from three to 50), keeping the living out of Hades and the dead within its boundaries.

J.K. Rowling included several significant dogs in the Harry Potter books, not least Fluffy, Hagrid's three-headed beast, and Fang his bloodhound. Virginia Woolf wrote the biography of Elizabeth Barrett Browning's Cocker Spaniel who 'represented the private side of life – the play side.'

Dogs have been used for comic relief in many long-lived books, Montmorency, the Fox Terrier in Jerome K. Jerome's *Three Men in a Boat* is possibly the most lovable of the book's characters, being more interested in fun and living life than his comic though self-obsessed human companions.

NICHOLSON'S
EST. 1873
DOG AND DUCK
EST. 1873
NICHOLSON'S
FREEHOUSE

Dogs and pubs

The Dog and Bear is a traditional British-style pub in Toronto, Canada. There was a pub of the same name in Nottingham, England. Bear baiting, which involved dogs being encouraged to attack a bear tied to a post, resulting in the inevitable gory mayhem, was banned as a sport in the 1830s.

The Dog and Doublet in Wolverhampton, England, may have derived its name from the clothing worn to identify hunters' retriever dogs. There are Dog and Trumpets pubs across the world, some like the one in Soho, London (now known as O'Neill's), named to celebrate 75 years of His Master's Voice record label.

There is a Dog Watch Tavern in Baltimore, USA, and there used to be several in the UK. The 'dog watch' was supposedly during the hours that the dogs were asleep, or between 4 and 6 pm and 6 and 8 pm. These short watches were used to help rotate the hours for the watchmen.

The Dog and Duck is a popular pub name for hunters and their retrievers; the one pictured is in London. There are others in the UK and Ireland, and across the world including Calgary, Canada, while Hawaii has the Dog and Duck Irish Pub.

Greyhounds

These beautiful well-tempered dogs are designed for high-speed pursuit and, over distance, will outpace and outlast any of the big cats. Greyhounds can run as fast as 45 miles/72 kilometres per hour over a quarter of a mile (400-metre) track.

Pairs of dogs used to race each other, chasing hares across fields. This became formalized and known as coursing and then Greyhound racing. A track was opened in Emeryville, California, in 1919 and a mechanical lure was used on the oval track. In the next decade, nearly 70 other tracks followed, and they quickly became centres for gambling.

The next decades saw Greyhound racing slowly gain legal recognition and sophisticated administration. In Australia, New Zealand, Ireland and the United Kingdom, Greyhound racing legislation is part of the gambling industry. However, it is frequently under attack by dog lovers, who find aspects of it unnecessary and sometimes cruel, and the sport may not endure indefinitely. Greyhound racing has significantly declined in the USA with, at the time of writing, just a few race tracks still running. It is illegal to bet on Greyhound racing in Canada.

Today, Greyhounds make calm, sweet family pets. Yes, they appreciate plenty of scope for exercise, but they are also surprisingly good at keeping the couch warm all day.

'We humans may be brilliant and we may be special, but we are still connected to the rest of life. No one reminds us of this better than our dogs.'

— Patricia B. McConnell

Dogs excluded from history books

In general, dogs get short changed in our written histories. We have been the best of friends for at least 8000 years, but try looking up dogs in the index of most history books: they are not there. It is as if there has been a hidden rule that serious history across the world only concerns humans and not their companions.

For example, the index of the great A.J.P. Taylor's *English History, 1914–1945* goes straight from 'Dockets' to (Admiral) 'Doenitz,' and Trevelyan's *History of England*'s index goes from 'District Council' straight to 'Domesday Book.' To be fair, Trevelyan's *English Social History*, published many years later, reported that politicians were complaining about the behaviour of the common man's dogs. In 1389, a statute decreed that 'No layman with less than forty shillings a year in land, and no priest or clerk with less than ten pounds income a year be so bold as to keep sporting nets or dogs.'

The statute was largely ignored. Trevelyan writes: 'The English were already notorious in Europe for their devotion to their horses and dogs of which they bred and kept many varieties in great numbers.'

‘I am his Highness’ dog at Kew; Pray tell me Sir, whose dog are you?’

— Alexander Pope

Mindfulness

'What is mindfulness? Perhaps the simplest way to describe it is to say that mindfulness is the practice of paying attention: knowing where our attention is, being able to choose where to direct it and being able to sustain it.'

— *Dr Craig Hassed,* Mindfulness For Life

'The animals are right here, right in front of us. And how we treat these companions is a test.'

— *Linda Blair*

Poodles

'I wonder if other dogs think poodles are members of a weird religious cult.'

— *Rita Rudner*

'Stotting is jumping upwards with all four legs simultaneously. My advice: do not die until you've seen a large black poodle stotting in the snow.'

— *Douglas Adams*

Poodles, the French National Dog (known as *Caniche*), come in all sorts of sizes including Standard Miniature and Toy, and humans have put poodles to work in all sorts of ways. Poodles can be strong, agile and intelligent, and easy to train. The Standard Poodle, in particular, is one of the world's most intelligent dogs, well known for being exceptionally observant.

Poodles were, for many years, mostly water-retrieval dogs, which is why the big Standard Poodles often have the swimming-efficient shaved-leg clip, and they also had a celebrated stint in the French Circus Industry. Today, you can find Poodles of all types in police forces and service roles.

In the early part of the last century, the Toy Poodle had a brief reputation as being the lap dog of the overly indulged rich housewife. Alan Ereira in his chapter on servants in his book, *The People's England*, reports a servant being told her duties by the lady of the house:

'My dear poodle can't eat meat

unless it's nicely minced. They must be washed every other day and combed every day; and the poodle must go for a walk when it's sunshiny, only you must never let him wet his feet but carry him across the street.'

Poodles may have once been synonymous with aristocratic-looking ladies walking in central Paris, but they have moved on from this rarified space to simply become loved, gentle family pets across much of the world. When socialized early, Poodles are wonderful with children and other animals.

Dog proverbs and sayings

Language is rich with sayings about dogs; here is a selection.
Speaking to Laertes, Shakespeare's Hamlet says that '**every dog has its day'**. Around 370 years later, Andy Warhol was quoted predicting everyone would have 'fifteen minutes of fame.'

'The dog days of summer' in the Roman era were named after Sirius, a dog-shaped star, that appeared in the sky in the warmest days of the season.

'Every dog is allowed one bite' — thereafter the dog's owner should know about his dog's propensity and is thereafter responsible for its behaviour in future.

'A dog's dinner' and **'A dog's breakfast'** are both sayings that mean little more than a mess — sometimes of organization, but more often of cooking that is deemed only fit for the dogs to eat. However, 'a dog's dinner' can also describe someone's overly gaudy style of dressing.

'Every dog is valiant at his own door' suggests that the further dogs — and by extension, people — are away from their comfort zone, the less brave they become.

'Doggo' can be an affectionate name for 'dog.' 'Lying doggo' is an old phrase for lying low and being concealed. However, as tame dogs are far from being good at this, it just might refer to their sometimes cautious and light sleep patterns.

'Going to the dogs.' Before the boom in pet food supplies, household dogs were generally fed what nobody wanted. The phrase has been extended to mean going to waste or ruin, and failure.

'Dog eat dog' indicates that the situation has become so competitive that people have little care or scruples about what they do, behaving as badly as if dogs were eating each other.

'Dogs wag their tails not so much in love to you as your bread' is a saying that has been attributed as far back as 1666, suggested that dogs are merely interested in you for the food you can offer.

'Dog fight': Tom Brokaw in his section with John Foss within the *Greatest Generation*, portrays just why this phrase is so apt: 'Those aerial battles were actually called dog fights, two snarling high-powered planes twisting and turning each trying to get the advantage ...'

'Hang dog' and '**hair of the dog'** probably relate to being **'sick as a dog'** — the 'hang dog' being the hangover and the 'hair' the cure!

'See a man about a dog' is a euphemism for going to the bathroom. It also used to mean a man seeing a woman for illicit purposes.

'Kiss the dog' is when a pickpocket goes face-to-face with his target, distracting them before stealing.

'Dog in a manger' refers to the cussed meanness of someone who has no use for something, but still prevents others from having it.

'Like a dog with two tails' is an expression indicating exceptional happiness.

'It's a dog's life' is a phrase that has kept pace with the times. It used to mean having a miserable time of life with scant food, affection and love. Nowadays, a dog's life is so much better than an ordinary dog's used to be, so today's dog's life is generally good.

White House dogs

The dogs in the White House are the world's highest profile pets. Their behaviour is under immense scrutiny and the choice of breed is highly influential for prospective dog owners. Though dealt with sparingly in most presidential biographies, the Presidential Pet Museum, with its own historian in residence, provides a wealth of information on its website.

The White House offers dogs plenty of people to care for them, lots of comfort, space and activity, and nearly all but the most energetic large animals seem to have enjoyed their time there. For their owners, who are typically very pressed for time, dogs offer instant friendship, company, entertainment, and a simple loyalty that does not otherwise come with the President's job.

Washington was a great dog lover and **Adams**, his vice President and successor (1797–1801), brought two dogs, Juno and Satan, with him into the White House. **Jefferson** (1801–1809), a great animal lover, had a Newfoundland and a Terrier with him. **James Monroe** (1817–1825) had a Siberian Husky. **John Tyler** (1841–1845) had a Greyhound and two Irish Wolfhounds. **Franklin Pierce** (1853–1857) kept a tiny dog, a gift from Japan known as a Chin. **James Buchanan**, the only bachelor President, had a Toy Terrier and a Newfoundland.

Abraham Lincoln (1861–1865) left his dog Fido at home, but took Jip, a small friendly dog who was often on his lap during meetings and meals in the White House.

Ulysses Grant (1869-1877) had two dogs with him: a Black-and-Tan named Rosie, and his daughter Jessie's Newfoundland named Faithful.

Rutherford Hayes (1877–1881) was

a great animal lover who kept eight dogs and addressed Congress on the need for better laws to protect animals. Hayes' dogs included an English Mastiff named Duke, a Newfoundland named Hector, a Greyhound named Grim, and Otis, a Miniature Schnauzer. President Garfield (1881) named his dog, a Newfoundland, Veto.

Grover Cleveland (1885–1889 and then again 1893–1897) had many dogs around him, including his wife Frances's French Poodle, Hector; a Spaniel, a Collie, and a big Saint Bernard called Kay, whose heft is reputed to have provided comfort to Frances. **Benjamin Harrison** (1889–1893) had a much-loved mixed-breed Collie, Dash, and is reputed to have had a Siberian Bloodhound as part of his White House entourage.

Theodore Roosevelt (1901–1909) kept a vast range of animals with him; reputedly his favourite dog was Pete the Bull Terrier, which lost his place in the White House after tearing the bottom out of the pants being worn by the French Ambassador. Another of Roosevelt's dogs was a Chesapeake Bay Terrier, Sailor Boy, who disturbingly loved gunpowder. In 1905, Roosevelt's daughter, Alice, was given a black Pekingese named Manchu by the Chinese Empress Cixi. Rollo was a friendly Saint Bernard and Skip, a hunting Terrier, even had a breed named after him: the Teddy Roosevelt Terrier.

William Taft (1909–1913) and his

wife Helen seemed to have preferred cows as pets to dogs. The singer Caruso thought a dog would be much more fun for the President's daughter; his gift of a little white dog was accepted and named Caruso. **Woodrow Wilson** (1913–1921) kept Davie, an Airedale Terrier. At the end of Wilson's second presidential term, he was given a very lovable and gentle white Bull Terrier named Bruce.

William Harding (1921–1923) also kept an Airedale Terrier, Laddie Boy. Harding understood newspapers and the power of the media, and Laddie Boy became a celebrity, with his own portrait — the original First Dog. Both Harding and his wife Florence campaigned for animal welfare and Laddie was the campaign's poster boy.

Calvin Coolidge (1923–1929) and First Lady Grace Coolidge were great animal lovers and had a considerable menagerie in their lives. Their White House years featured several white

Collies including the playful Rob Roy and Prudence Prim. The half-brother of President Harding's Laddie Boy earned the name Paul Pry for his constant puppy-like curiosity. As the American Kennel Club describes on their website, Airedale Terriers 'won't back down when protecting hearth and home' and several White House staffers were nipped and bitten by Paul Pry before he was assigned to the Marines.

Paul Pry wasn't the only dog in the Coolidge pack that caused trouble. The aptly named Calamity Jane was a white Shetland Sheepdog who was keen on getting messy. Calamity needed special cleaning arrangements, and though the

Coolidges did increase the popularity of 'Shelties', the public quickly learned to seek dogs that were not pure white.

Herbert Hoover (1929–1933) campaigned using a photograph of him and his Belgian Shepherd, King Tut, which he acquired while in Europe managing food relief after the First World War. Though a successful man, Hoover was unknown in the USA and it was thought that an image of a benign-looking man with a dog could generate broad appeal. After Hoover's election, King Tut found White House living stressful and started to sadly fade away. Pat, a German Shepherd, replaced King Tut and similarly patrolled the grounds. Weegie, a Norwegian Elkhound, came at around the time Pat did and, like Pat, retired with the Hoovers to Palo Alto. The Hoovers had several other dogs, including Collies and a Siberian Husky.

Franklin D. Roosevelt's (1933–1945) dog, Fala, a black Scotch Terrier, was a regular companion and is often photographed with Roosevelt. Fala has a statue at Roosevelt's Washington Memorial. During his many years in the White House, several other dogs took up residence, including Winks, a Llewellin Setter, and a Great Dane named President.

Harry S. Truman (1945–1953) and his family 'preferred to be pet-free' and gave away the Cocker Spaniel puppy gifted to them by an admirer. The cute puppy's pictures had been spread across the nation and reputedly thousands of people wrote in angry protest.

Dwight D. Eisenhower (1953–1961) kept a Weimaraner, Heidi, who after an indiscretion with an expensive rug, was exiled from the White House and took up permanent residence on the family farm.

John F. Kennedy (1961–1963) was a great dog lover and came to the White House with Charlie, his much-beloved Welsh Terrier. In total, there were as many as nine dogs at one time in the White House under the Kennedys including Pushinka, a gift from Khruschev, who produced puppies with Charlie.

The White House Kennel Keeper at the time, Traphes Bryant, recalled that Kennedy called for Charlie's company at the height of the Cuban Missile Crisis.

Lyndon B. Johnson (1963–1969) loved Beagles and two of them, Him and Her, became national celebrities and were included in many of the White House's activities.

Richard H. Nixon (1969–1974) kept in the White House a French Poodle, a Yorkshire Terrier and an Irish Setter. **Gerald Ford** (1974–1977) kept Golden Retrievers, one of whom, Liberty, became well-known and loved across the USA after giving birth to nine puppies. **James (Jimmy) Carter** (1977–1981) kept a Border Collie-mix called Grits for two years, and Lewis Brown, an Afghan Hound.

Ronald Reagan (1981–1989), along with Nancy, was a great animal lover, but all but two of their dogs stayed on their ranch. Lucky was given to Nancy as a puppy and grew 'from a ball of fluff to the size of a pony.' Lucky was

a Belgian herding dog, a Bouvier des Flandres, who, being big, powerful and boisterous, eventually outgrew the constraints of the White House. Rex, a Cavalier King Charles Spaniel, came next, with a bundle of energy and enthusiasm for White House life.

George H.W. Bush (1989–1993) kept a Springer spaniel, Millie, who 'wrote' a bestselling book describing her life at the White House. Millie's son, Ranger, bonded very closely with the President and was frequently with him.

William (Bill) J. Clinton (1993–2001) had Buddy, a chocolate Labrador Retriever, join him for his second term because 'he wanted one loyal friend in Washington.'

George W. Bush (2001–2009) kept Spot, the son of George H.W.'s dog Millie, and a couple of Scottish Terriers, Miss Beazley and Barney, whose friendship and ball-playing antics made them popular with the public.

Barack H. Obama (2009–2017) kept two Portuguese Water Dogs, Bo and later his sister Sunny. Spirited and full of character, these two dogs epitomized the loving family nature the Obama White House years projected.

Donald Trump (2017–2021) didn't keep any pets, citing lack of time as the reason.

Joseph (Joe) Biden is known for his love of German Shepherds. Champ had served with Biden in his vice-presidential years and made it with him to the White House in 2001. Major, the first rescue dog to be in the White House, was also a German Shepherd. A third, Commander, was rehomed away from the White House after a few reported biting incidents.

‘I think we are drawn to dogs because they are the uninhibited creatures we might be if we weren’t certain we knew better.’

— George Bird Evans

Saluki

There is at least 5000 years' evidence of the Saluki breed in remnants of ancient Egypt, Greece, Persia and the Middle East. Considered a royal dog of Egypt, mummified Salukis have been found in the Upper Nile Pyramids.

Fast, graceful, narrow-headed and with soft ears, these loving but reserved dogs have contributed their hunting prowess and elegance to the Middle East and are also sought after in the West.

Though sometimes stubborn and requiring extensive training, the Saluki can be a joy to their owner. The Crown Prince of Dubai, Sheikh Hamdan bin Mohammed Al Maktoum released happy videos walking his rescued Saluki, Grace, who seemed to be quickly and positively responding to his attentions.

Most dogs hunt by smell and sound, but Salukis hunt by sight and their speed can match a Greyhound's.

A DOG
ATE MY
TAX RETURNS

Dog tax and registration: When a dog tax nearly started a war

The need to have a dog registered and licensed is well understood in much of the world as a way to ensure that strays are managed and dog owners are held accountable for their animal's behaviour. Globally, the trend is to ensure that all dogs are microchipped and that the chip itself becomes the licence.

There is some historical baggage to deal with, however. In some regional jurisdictions, collection of a dog fee or tax has less to do with the dog's welfare than the collectors' or their employer's benefits. This can also do a massive disservice to professional dog catchers, who are generally wanting more resources and are motivated by animal welfare.

Britain had a tax on dogs between 1796 and 1882, and this probably gave authorities in New Zealand the idea to impose a dog tax from 1890. In the north of the country in Hokianga, the local council decided to determinedly impose the tax in 1898. The region's population was predominately Māori who, by and large, were not involved in the cash economy. For them, the tax was both discriminatory and a symbol of an oppressive Crown. Their leaders decided to fight and made full preparations. The Crown sent a small force that ran away and then sent a much larger contingent ready for a flown-blown battle. Only desperate and last-moment diplomacy by the Hon. Hene, the Member of Parliament for Northern Māori averted bloodshed.

The Dachshund

The Eastern Canadian Dachshund Club quotes on its website the author Delinger, from his 1947 book, *The Complete Dachshund*: 'It is frequently said — and truly — that any person having once owned a Dachshund will never care to be without at least one representative of the breed.'

Sometimes almost pugnacious with strangers, affectionate with owners and children, and always agile active and curious, the Dachshund's popularity is growing:

'His size makes him suitable to the small, modern home and the Miniature varieties may be kept without inconvenience even in small flats ... his high intelligence, loyalty, unfailing sense of humour and adaptability endear him to all who have the good fortune to know him intimately.'

— E. Fitch Daglish from The Popular Dachshund

The Dachshund gained breed status with the American Kennel Club in 1885, which recognized three coat varieties: smooth, wire- and long-haired. They also come in many colours: fawn, black, chocolate, cream, red and blue.

Maisie, a Wire-haired Dachshund, won the Crufts Best Of Show Award in 2020 and had a much-televised quick poo during her victory lap.

Big dog shows

England's famous Crufts Dog Show was founded in 1891 and claims to be 'the world's greatest dog show.' New York's Westminster Dog Show was established in 1877 and claims to be America's second-most-watched sporting show. Both shows are concerned with breed standards, and prizes are awarded to the dogs who best represent those standards. They are enormous events requiring complex and sophisticated administration, high-calibre management teams, plus a host of volunteers. Thousands of people and dogs attend and the TV audiences run into many millions.

Dog shows originated in agricultural presentations in the early nineteenth century. Soon after, presentations by breed originated and kennel clubs have been cementing standards and running shows ever since. Right across the world, there are frequent dog shows organized by breed or sometimes just by geography. One of the most famous is Alberta's, with their Kennel Club claiming to have the biggest outdoor dog show in Canada with around 3000 dogs competing.

While the majority of dog lovers are not interested in showing their animals, the kennel clubs and breeders concerned do much for the preservation and well-being of known breeds. They also demonstrate just how much joy can be shared between humans and well-trained dogs. The Westminster and Crufts' winners of the highly coveted 'Best in Show awards' bring prime-time world news coverage to themselves and their breeds.

Animal shelters

Animal shelters reveal the worst of the human condition and also show it at its best. Abandoned, neglected, discarded and dumped dogs end up in shelters around the world in staggering numbers.

The World Animal Foundation's website relays that: 'Every year over 6.3 million dogs and cats and other household pets are surrendered to animal shelters. Sadly, just over 4 million find a home every year leaving an ever-increasing number of animals in the shelter population.'

The only good news here is that millions *are* rescued and those who work in shelters, often volunteer with the tiniest of budgets, make extraordinary efforts to care for their charges. Great institutions like Britain's Battersea Dogs and Cats Home, founded in 1860, have expanded to meet growing needs. As well as now running three of its own sites, Battersea runs an academy to help train people running other rescue institutions, and other major efforts are directed towards improving people's knowledge of pet care and needs.

Most areas across Britain, America, Canada, Australia and New

Zealand will have an active animal welfare charity, be it a humane society, a Blue Cross, SPCA or similar, or a local organization. Many of these have a no-kill policy. However, on a daily average basis, over a thousand dogs in shelters are euthanized. How did it come to this?

Over half of all dogs are euthanized because of their levels of aggression and untreatable injuries. Covid lockdowns drove many around the world to add a pet to their household. Sometimes this did not work out well. In other cases, people went back to their old lives, not allowing time for, and losing interest in, keeping their pets. In a way, this was akin to a large-scale enactment of the post-Christmas rejection of puppies, when the delight in them can turn into rejection due to the commitment and costs involved. Clearly, the privilege and responsibility of owning dogs is not always thought about as much as it should be. It is the humans that let the dogs down, not the other way around.

Post-Covid, the trends are improving for dogs, yet animal shelters everywhere remain in need of resources.

References

Books

Isabelle Duff and Susannah Crispe, *Cookie*
John Bradshaw, *Dog Sense: How the new science of dog behaviour can make you a better friend to your pet*
Susan Orlean, *Rin Tin Tin: The life and legend*
The Bible, Philippians 3:2
The Bible, Psalms 22:16–19
Assoc. Prof. Craig Hassed & Dr Stephen Mckenzie, *Mindfulness for Life*
William George Smith, *The Oxford Dictionary of English Proverbs*
Alan Ereira, *The People's England*
Tom Brokaw, *The Greatest Generation*

News sources

Daily Telegraph (Australia)
ABC News (Australia)
The Guardian (UK)
NDTV
The Globe and Mail

Organizations & Websites

American Kennel Club: https://www.akc.org/
Sanford Health: https://www.sanfordhealth.org/
The Human Animal Bond Research Institute (HABRI): https://habri.org/
American Veterinary Medical Association: https://www.avma.org/
The Fi Collar blog: https://blog.tryfi.com/how-long-do-labs-live/
Dogster: https://www.dogster.com/
Farmer-ish: https://farmerish.net/
dvm360: https://www.dvm360.com/view/eczema-asthma-and-the-protective-effect-of-dogs
Business Insider: https://www.businessinsider.com/photos-show-sea-dogs-serving-alongside-sailors-navy-2023-12#dogs-have-been-part-of-the-us-navy-since-its-inception-3
Hill's Pet: https://www.hillspet.co.nz/dog-care/dog-breeds/portuguese-water-dog
Mayo Clinic Health System: https://www.mayoclinichealthsystem.org/hometown-health/speaking-of-health/dogs-are-good-for-your-health
American Heart Association: https://www.heart.org/en/healthy-living/healthy-bond-for-life-pets/pet-owners/a-dog-could-be-good-for-your-heart
Barking Mad: https://www.barkingmad.uk.com/
Get Set Pet: https://www.getsetpet.com/blogs/news/why-every-office-should-have-a-dog?_pos=1&_sid=fda41fa5e&_ss=r

Daily Paws: https://www.dailypaws.com/dogs-puppies/dog-safety-tips/how-to-pet-dog#:~:text=%22If%20the%20dog%20shows%20an,pet%20her%20shoulder%20or%20chest.%22&text=Always%20avoid%20reaching%20over%20the,see%20how%20the%20dog%20reacts

Petsmont: https://www.petsmont.com/blogs/pets/how-to-pet-a-dog-techniques-and-other-important-tips

Wag!: https://wagwalking.com/breed/top-dog-breeds-that-will-protect-you

The Spruce Pets: https://www.thesprucepets.com/

Cesar: https://www.cesar.com/dog-care/socialization/when-dogs-become-mans-best-friends#:~:text=It's%20estimated%20that%20about%2015%2C000,associate%20more%20closely%20with%20humans

Deans Services: https://www.deansservices.com/termite-treatment

Auburn University: https://www.auburn.edu/main/auburninspires/feature/auburndog/

Canada Border Services Agency: https://www.cbsa-asfc.gc.ca/security-securite/dds-scd/menu-eng.html

Australian Border Force: https://www.abf.gov.au/about-us/what-we-do/border-protection/detector-dogs/breeding#:~:text=Detector%20dog%20%80%8B%E2%80%8B%E2%80%8BOur%20breeding,are%20highly%20driven

NZ Detector Dogs: https://www.nzdetectordogs.co.nz/?gclid=C-j0KCQiA2eKtBhDcARIsAEGTG-43Cx-31n8k17qxhp9UFmLzGx6jMS7F-1qiEB-Pusokra5P7lRfiOWzYaAphIEALw_wcB

Famous Dogs in History: https://dogs-in-history.blogspot.com/2020/04/kostya-russias-faithful-dog.html

British Dalmatian Club: https://www.britishdalmatianclub.org.uk/

Dalmatian Club of Victoria: https://www.dalmatianclubofvictoria.com.au/

Purina: https://www.purina.com/dogs/dog-breeds/australian-shepherd-dog-breed

Grey2K USA Worldwide: https://www.grey2kusa.org/about/history.php#:~:text=The%20history%20of%20greyhound%20racing,the%20Blue%20Star%20Amusement%20Company.

Presidential Pet Museum: https://www.presidentialpetmuseum.com/whitehousepets-1/

World Animal Foundation: https://worldanimalfoundation.org/

Also in this series

Also in the Animal Happiness series

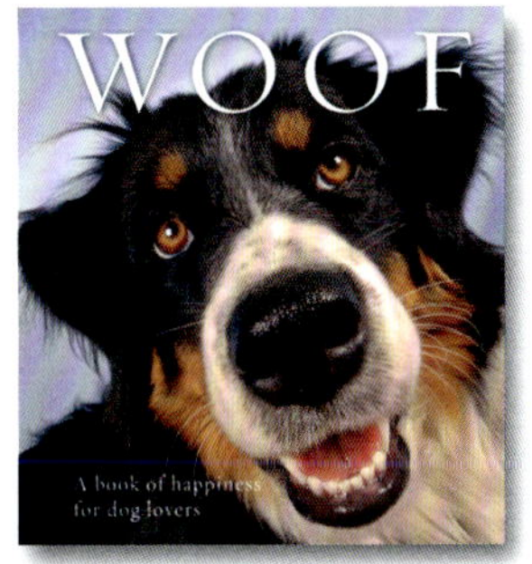

First published 2024
This edition published 2025

Exisle Publishing Pty Ltd
PO Box 864, Chatswood, NSW 2057, Australia
226 High Street, Dunedin, 9016, New Zealand
www.exislepublishing.com

A CiP record for this book is available from the National Library of Australia.

ISBN 978-1-923011-22-9

Designed by Mark Thacker
Typeset in Accumin Pro Light 11 on 16pt
Photographs courtesy of Shutterstock, with the exception of the Avalanche dog photograph on page 75 courtesy of Jane Dunn Photography
Printed in China

This book uses paper sourced under ISO 14001 guidelines from well-managed forests and other controlled sources.

2 4 6 8 10 9 7 5 3 1